gratitude

& grace

✦

a divine guide
for being human

✦

Indigo Sky

Core: *Love. Inspire. Value. Educate.*

Gratitude & Grace includes ideas based on interpretation of mystical principles, tarot and cognitive learning principles as they relate to behavioral patterns. These ideas have been prepared by Indigo Sky in a way that can be implemented into daily life, if you choose. To learn more about Indigo Sky, turn to page 127.

Tarot Cards have historical significance as a popular card game as well as being used for divination for centuries. The *Sola-Busca Tarot*, known to be used in the 15th Century in Italy, served as part of the inspiration for A.E. Waite to co-create the *Rider-Waite Tarot*, which was published in the early 1900's. Over time, many variations of tarot have emerged. One of the most popular tarot decks today is the *Universal Waite Tarot*. Other popular decks include *The Thoth Tarot, The Good Tarot, Angel Tarot Cards, Fairy Tarot Cards, Deviant Moon Tarot, The Akashic Tarot* and many more.

Disclaimer

Dedication

This project is dedicated to the idea that we can change everything in an instant and begin anew.

Prayer for my Mother

May you find joy in any breath.
May the strength of God lift you.
May you see miracles in any moment.
May your heart be as soft as the morning sun.
May you be tender and kind with yourself.
May you be guided by God, if it is to be.
May you gently step through each day.
May you know Divine Wellness
and enjoy Unconditional Love.

Amen.

Appreciation & Gratitude

I wish to express my special thanks to an incredible team of mighty companions. You are among my angels here on Earth.

I will continue to do my best to ensure that the many people who have been so helpful know how grateful I am for their kindness, love, compassion and friendship.

✦

My glass is half full.
My glass is half empty.
I am so grateful for the water
in my glass.

✦

Moment of Grace

Daily Prayer

May I be guided into the Light within me
and energized by the wisdom around me.

May I be reminded how truly grateful I am
for the kindness of so many people
throughout this lifetime.

Some know it, yet others do not.
Unfortunately, a few may never know it.
May I be reminded to forgive myself,
as I am learning as I go.

Thank you.

May I allow myself to be guided
by the Divine force that created me,
for that is where I can find Truth.

Where I perceive barriers, may they
be dissolved to allow Love to
flow freely into my open heart.

As I seek, may I be reminded to look within.

May I continually find the strength to center
my thoughts, my heart, my soul, my being.

And so, it is.

How can I **appreciate** this moment **even more**
while releasing attachment to any outcome?

Who can I be in this moment?

Contents

Foreword   11
Guide to the Guide   12

1	I Allow	14		27	I am Tranquil	66
2	I am Peaceful	16		28	I am Wise	68
3	I am Loving	18		29	I am Youthful	70
4	I am Grateful	20		30	I am Worthy	72
5	I am Gracious	22		31	I am Caring	74
6	I am Beautiful	24		32	I am Open	76
7	I am Light	26		33	I am Creative	78
8	I am Generous	28		34	I am One	80
9	I am Able	30		35	I am Sweet	82
10	I am Joyful	32		36	I Appreciate	84
11	I am Centered	34		37	I am Tender	86
12	I am Courageous	36		38	I am Gentle	88
13	I am Happy	38		39	I am Warm	90
14	I am Kind	40		40	I am Bright	92
15	I am Honest	42		41	I am Valuable	94
16	I am Hopeful	44		42	I am Well	96
17	I am Resourceful	46		43	I am Trustworthy	98
18	I am Inspired	48		44	I am Whole	100
19	I am Forgiving	50		45	I am Authentic	102
20	I am Thankful	52		46	I am a Unifier	104
21	I am Flexible	54		47	I am Friendly	106
22	I am Mighty	56		48	I am Disciplined	108
23	I am Honorable	58		49	I am Balanced	110
24	I am Resilient	60		50	I am Effective	112
25	I am Magnetic	62		51	I am Illustrious	114
26	I am Soulful	64		52	I am Optimistic	116
					I am Radiant	118

Farewell & Closing this Sacred Circle   118
The Greatest Moments   121
Ways to Help   123
Step Forward in Love   124
Mighty Companions Preview   125
Mindful Adventures   126
Origin of Indigo Sky   127
References   129

This book belongs to

_____

20 _ _

foreword

"Those who bring sunshine into the lives of others cannot keep it from themselves."

Mother.

Rua Louise
February second, 1936.

"Those who bring sunshine into the lives of others cannot keep it from themselves."

Sir James Matthew Barrie, 1st Baronet, OM
Scottish Novelist & Playwright
Creator of Peter Pan

A note from my lovely great-grandmother Rua Louise, written to her 10-year old daughter, my adorable grandmother Helen Louise.

GUIDE TO THE GUIDE

Gratitude & Grace is a self-study guide, created through an exploration of tarot, intuition and inspiration to offer a year of uplifting messages, activities and daily reminders for a wonderful day. It is unbound by traditional restraints to create an inspiring and beautiful journey for anyone who participates. You may begin on any day that feels right for you. Create your own mindful adventures by flipping to any page or date and see what messages emerge for you. Try it!

The Soulful Sketchbook has been designed for you to express yourself as you wish. Think of the space up top as your personal vision board, story boards or simply a place to doodle and play. The journal below has been designed as a simple way to begin with a few drops of wisdom to draw upon as you grow. Each chapter includes quotes, an affirmation and self-reflective questions. For anyone who is left-handed, reverse the book for a more comfortable journaling experience if you wish.

You may notice repetitive patterns in the book. Just as in life, messages may repeat themselves. Patterns that grab your attention are a call to action!

Inspiration for this project began on January 11 as I believe it is the beginning of a significant mystical cycle. You can test it out - instead of beginning your resolutions on New Year's Day, spend January 1-10 preparing, then begin on January 11. See if it makes it easier to stick with your new goals!

✗ This symbol, at the top right of each chapter, indicates your affirmative power thought for the week. This is a simple way to enhance your day in one second flat!

∞ This symbol appears beside the date when an activity is mentioned. If you wish to practice an activity, this symbol means there is *(or will be)* additional tools/content on **IndigoSkylab.com** to help guide you further.

♥ This symbol appears on some dates when a tragedy occurred. Visit page 123 for ways to honor lives lost, contribute and remain engaged for ongoing support.

Please take from this thought-provoking guide whatever you like, leave the rest. Resist the urge to dwell upon one message over another. It, like a full life, consists of many ideas, including your own wisdom. Remain focused on aligning with your loving heart and peaceful mind and allow yourself to be guided toward a light, bright future.

Om

Chapter One

Morning Affirmation

May I be reminded to begin my day with gratitude and grace. Everything I seek is already within me. May I stay connected to unconditional love, beautiful healing light and the abundance of miracles and blessings that surround me. May each breath bring joy.

January 1 - January 10

Messages for early January appear on page 116 and 118.

January 11

Magic and miracles await you! Imagine yourself as a magic wand, connected with an infinite flow of light, here on Earth to delight us with your most sacred expressions of love. Dive deep into your heart and your dreams. Breathe. Take a leap of faith and allow miracles to manifest through you. To begin, say "I allow, I am willing."

January 12

Continue the great work you wish to create. Keep yourself open to miracles. This path you have set forth suits you. Give love and your heart will always be full.

January 13   ∞

Where things have not lived up to your expectations, take the lessons and move on. Sit quietly. Meditate so that you may refine things from a higher place. Ask for guidance and listen, with patience, for the answers. Tend to your heart to allow a bright future. Allowing is an art form. When done well, it crafts a masterpiece that empowers you to master peace.

14 January 15

"Imagination creates reality."   "Life is a process to be enjoyed."

Richard Wagner   Abraham Hicks

Soulful Sketchbook

When any heart opens, we are all lifted.

Create your core. Make a list of loving, mindful activities. Repeat often.
What else can you do right now to treat yourself with care?

Chapter Two

January 16

When you perceive an imbalance in the world, you may wish to act. Trust your intuition. If you are compelled toward anything specific, lean into it. Take action. What do you believe in? What do you stand for? What will you not stand for?

January 17

As you observe yourself and humanity, acknowledge any problems without getting stuck in the mud. Take a step back to lift yourself above it all. Explore the problems without taking them personally. What else could it mean? Ask for easy-to-interpret signs. Ask for Divine solutions, then listen with an open heart and an open mind. Remain connected to the Divine part of you through full, deep measured breath.

January 18

A life of enchantment finds you when you connect with your creativity and passion. You are on the right path. Periods of constriction show us our strength and allow us to be grateful for our place within this incredible rhythm of life on Earth. As a creative alternative to conflict, practice being delightful.

January 19

As you balance the light and the dark within you, remember that you are a bringer of light. When you notice darkness, turn on your light. Seek harmony and it will be.

January 20

We get what we focus on, not what we want. Wishes are granted to those who ask. What is most important to you? How do you wish to express yourself? Who do you wish to become? Ask for miracles and you may receive.

21 January 22

"The ultimate source of comfort and peace is within ourselves."

"Peace begins with a smile."

Dalai Lama

Mother Teresa

Soulful Sketchbook

Refine yourself by how you define yourself.

What are your strengths? What are your most wonderful qualities?
How do you define yourself? Start with 'I am _____'

wisdom journal

Chapter Three

January 23

Be generous with your heart and do anything you can to help others. A healthy, open heart yields great wealth. Take time today to enjoy a touch of your great wealth.

January 24

You hold the key to unlocking the mysteries of the Universe, as anyone does. Instead of waiting for a knight in shining armor, we must become the knight and help one another, united for good.

January 25   ∞

Let clarity find you through your willingness to be found. You need not get too confused. Align with your intuition, tap into your feelings and become aware of what you are being called to do. From a place of love, begin taking peaceful action. These are the loving first steps into exploring the light. The way forward is only revealed through deep, loving breath.

January 26

You are a gentle, loving, kind and compassionate contribution to the world. Your heightened sensitivity, when left unattended, may leave you stuck in the shadows. But you know better. Change your lens and refocus. What you can do to glow today? Lift yourself, lift others. Add light.

January 27

You are among the protectors of this wonderful planet. As you take simple steps to care for others, remember to take great care of yourself. Fill your heart with love. We all need you to be well. Embrace the idea that we are here on official business, elected from the ether to come to Earth to learn, grow, bloom and glow.

28 January 29

"Education is the kindling of a flame,   "Everything is either an expression
        not the filling of a vessel."   of love, or a call for love."

Socrates   A Course in Miracles

Soulful Sketchbook

May the light within your heart soften any resistance to love.

Send anyone you love a simple text message with a heart emoji.
First, write a love note to yourself.

Chapter Four

January 30

Uncertainty is simply a call to action. To see clearly, close your eyes. Look beyond the Earthly plane to connect with the infinite flow of love, light and life all around you. From darkness, a new dawn will emerge, as it always does. Be willing to accept help graciously. Use it wisely and for great things. Step forward in love. Leap with faith.

January 31   ∞

Change can be so painful and yet so joyful. We are here to create and relate, regardless of day-to-day emotional variances. Get yourself outside in nature, at sunrise or sunset or under the stars, disconnect from tech and enjoy a cosmic status update.

February 01

We are linked by how we think. In the moments where you allow yourself to cherish your prosperity, miracles will continue to flow through you and to you. Enjoy this moment from a place of gratitude.

February 02

Maturity is a development of life to be appreciated. Allow yourself to grow each day. Society, as it exists today, is simply our inheritance from our elders and peers. We can repeat their experience, we can improve upon it or we can completely change it. Ride the emotional waves as they come, until you learn how to soar above them. You are wise beyond your years. Let yourself be guided by good.

February 03

Sometimes it feels like we are characters in an epic adventure filled with seemingly endless chaos. Every story needs great heroes to inspire us. Helping others is truly heroic. Empower yourself to lend a hand. Stand in the strength of your heart and the grace of your light. Where can you be of service? What can you offer?

04 February 05

"Gratitude is not only the greatest of virtues, but the parent of all others."

Gracias. Mahalo. Merci. Asante. Arigato. Takk. Dankie. Grazie.

Cicero

Eight Ways to Say Thank You

Soulful Sketchbook

Count your money only once you count your blessings.

List 8 things for which you are grateful. These will be your grateful eight. You can update them as often as you wish.

Chapter Five

February 06 ∞

You are a conductor of charisma, but a visionary without harmony doesn't see well. As you grow into a well-balanced leader, remember that with great power comes an equal level of responsibility. Develop your core strength. Act with care to prevent a fall from grace.

February 07 ∞

Sometimes the train falls off the track and plans radically change. When things go off course, take a moment to mourn the plan that fell apart. Allow yourself room to heal and grow. Shift your focus to ask for the lesson. See the light in any darkness and allow something great to come to you. Develop your practice of mindful breathing.

February 08

Strengthen your connection to the love and light within you by choosing love above all. Guide yourself back to nirvana and stay there. In any moment when you are unable to see love, recognize it as an opportunity to dive deep into your compassionate heart. You have the great capacity to give love. Give love graciously.

February 09

Pause. Take a deep breath. And another. And another. Think about everyone around you, the ones you know along with everyone else. Imagine yourself surrounded with beautiful, healing light. Imagine each being inside a bubble of light, gently gliding along. Love is needed, everywhere, always. Blast everyone with love.

February 10

Resist the urge to run away from tough situations and instead, take the opportunity to draw upon your wisdom to learn and grow. If you get swept out of alignment, remain calm until you are able to snap yourself back in.

11 February 12

"I will hold myself to a standard of grace, not perfection."

"If you chase two rabbits, you will not catch either one."

Emily Ley

Russian Proverb

Soulful Sketchbook

wisdom doodles

Your creativity will take you far.
Cultivating creativity in others will take you farther.

Think of a moment where you overreacted and re-imagine it.
Now, rewrite the scene, act with grace and create a new path.

wisdom journal

Chapter Six

February 13

Peace begins and ends with each and every one of us. Each moment when we realize we are more alike than not, we are closer to peace. Peace is a choice, your choice. Be willing to practice peace.

February 14

Imagine a single beam of light coming from the Universe down to Earth to fill your heart and soul with love. Try it. Place your hands over your heart, close your eyes and imagine you are being filled with light. By doing so, you may attract other beautiful heart-centric, soul-centric people to you. Send light and love around the world and together, we all rise.

February 15

Self-doubt is part of the human experience. Trust the sacred force, the sacred source, that created you and you will no longer seek the approval of others.

February 16

During your brief visit to Earth, enjoy learning anything you can. Immerse yourself in a new area, master a trade, become an expert. However, if you notice your head inflating a bit too much, keep yourself grounded through your open and loving heart.

February 17

In moments when you feel you are unable to receive love, may you be reminded that an infinite flow of love always surrounds you. As love flows to you, embrace it with open arms, while releasing attachment to it. Allow it to expand within you and lift you up. Be willing to receive love.

18 February 19

"The greatest gift you can ever give another person is your own happiness."

"I saw the angel in the marble and carved until I set him free."

Abraham Hicks

Michaelangelo

Soulful Sketchbook

wisdom doodles

Approach anyone who may offer help
with appreciation and gratitude.

What do you consider to be beautiful? How do you define beauty?
Do you know how beautiful you are?

wisdom journal

Chapter Seven

February 20

In our youth and teens, our emotions often fluctuate out of control. As we mature, if we mature, we learn to measure the cadence of our emotional capacity. When you discover your rhythm, you can dance through each day as if it has been choregoraphed for your prosperity. What moves you?

February 21

To navigate from confusion or chaos to clarity, imagine a radiant source of golden light finding its way, through any darkness, all the way down to you. The light can find you anywhere at any time, if you allow. Breathe and invite luminous ideas to come through you and thus, to you. Close your eyes and enjoy a moment of peace, filled with love and light. A spark of inspiration is all it takes to set forth on a bright path.

February 22

Explorers bring passion and excitement wherever they go. Explore the world around you with child-like wonder. Embrace the passion that comes from the confident expression of your youthful spirit.

February 23   ∞

If things feel out of balance, take a step back to explore the intentions and integrity of those around you. Look at yourself as well. Examine the influence you have on others and evaluate the influence they have on you. Is there cause for concern or can you rise above? Teach yourself to respond only when you understand what motivates you.

February 24   ∞

If you feel overwhelmed, stop what you are doing! Center yourself through slow, controlled breath. Take a break. Take a walk. Ground yourself. These wonderful things coming your way are to be enjoyed! Find a lighter path where you feel less resistance or none at all.

25 February 26

"L'chaim!"   "Live in the sunshine, swim
~ To Life! ~   the sea, drink the wild air."

Hebrew Toast   Ralph Waldo Emerson

Soulful Sketchbook

Bathe in the gentle sunlight
to soften any shadows upon your heart.

What are your favorite things to do to lift yourself to
your happy place? What adventures await you?

Chapter Eight

February 27   ∞

To link your attention with your breath, close your eyes and imagine yourself in a serene place. Notice each inhale and exhale. Allow peaceful, deep breathing with the intent to calm your mind and open your heart. When faced with tough decisions, re-create this sacred space of awareness, educate yourself wholly and only then decide.

February 28

At times, our light appears much brighter. Trust your perceptive abilities and reflect upon the light within. In darkness, faith allows you to maintain an intuitive orbit, knowing the light will return. Let fears fade into light as they float away, for life is ever-evolving.

✎ February 29 ✎

As a bringer of fire and light, you can see what others cannot. Your perceptive insights are among your greatest gifts. Let them flow freely, with glee, to lift us to a level of excitement we don't often see!

March 01

Success follows a framework that you can adopt at any time. Strive to be a valuable role model and it will be. You have the support of everything that lives and breathes as well as the Divine source that created it all. We all want you to be well and do well. What could you do to craft a strong foundation for your continued success?

March 02

Pure luck is heavenly. As you fortify your foundation with a mindset for miracles, you can allow an incredible rush of luck.

March 03

Each day, you are becoming the foremost leading expert of YOU! One critical thing to always remember, without gratitude, all could be lost. Celebrate this moment and enjoy your progress!

04 March 05

"The sun, with all those planets revolving around it and dependent on it, can still ripen a bunch of grapes as if it had nothing else in the universe to do."

"You, yourself, as much as anybody in the entire universe, deserve your love and affection."

Galileo Galilei   Buddha

Soulful Sketchbook

wisdom doodles

Offer to pay one bill for a family member or friend,
if you should find yourself so fortunate.

List teeny-tiny ideas for being kind and generous and see if you can
do them tomorrow. Or better yet, start with you and start today!

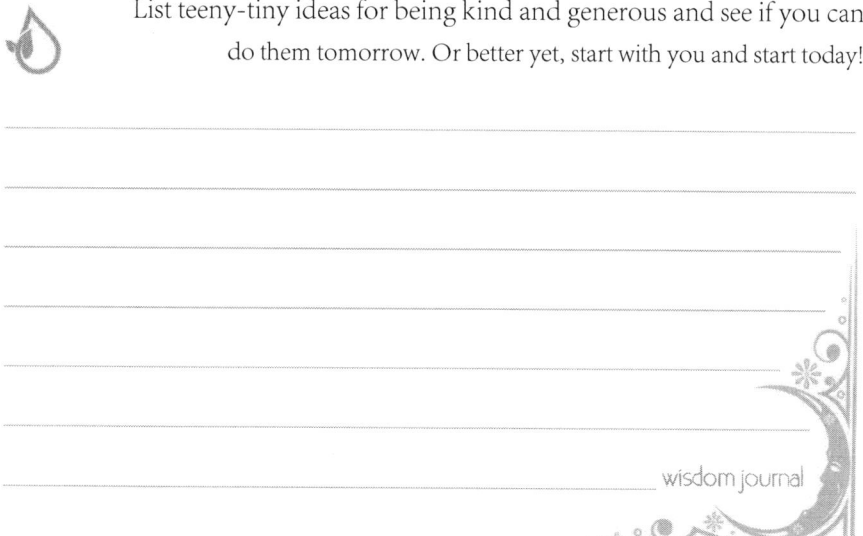

wisdom journal

Chapter Nine

March 06 ∞

We are wired with an electrical system so complex, sometimes it feels as though a jump start may be needed. Enjoy a spark of inspiration from wherever it may come, notably when it stirs the depths of your soul. Find a nice set of soulful jumper cables to electrify your life! In other words, what are some things you could do to power up?

March 07

Sometimes it is best not to share everything with everyone. If you choose to express your soul to another, approach with a youthful, light-hearted spirit. Remain unattached to any outcome, otherwise your passion and intensity could have a reverse effect. Ask 'How can I explore my sacred gifts, free from care?' Listen for the answers.

March 08 ∞

Continue taking excellent care of yourself so that you may take great care of others. Self-care is the opposite of being selfish. Plan quiet time for self-reflection to help heal thyself. Create a mystical cocoon to set the tone for a miraculous transformation. Your wings are almost ready. Trust the process.

March 09

When you emerge from your sacred space, remain centered as you engage and interact with others who are sharing this world. Explore with an open mind to find groups where you feel you belong.

March 10

Grace is the lost art of mercy. We need you to lead with unconditional love. Soften your heart, spread your wings and extend your good will to everyone. Speak softly, step lightly, act with kindness, passion, confidence and grace. Merci!

11 March 12

"Every great dream begins with a dreamer. Always remember, you have within you the strength, the patience, and the passion to reach for the stars to change the world."

Harriet Tubman

"I do not feel obligated to believe that the same God who has endowed us with sense, reason, and intellect has intended us to forgo their use."

Galileo Galilei

Soulful Sketchbook

When you see a parent traveling with children,
lend a hand and a prayer.

What are your greatest passions, dreams, desires?
What are the first steps to take you closer to them?

Chapter Ten

March 13

As a guardian of grace, you are entrusted with the sacred gift of leadership. When people look to you for guidance, trust your intuition. In robust stillness, you will emerge as a role model. Be quiet, peaceful and calm and the way forward will be shown to you.

March 14   ∞

Our visit to Earth is a brief, delightful engagement. One of the most powerful ideas you can entertain is a willingness to learn the art of forgiveness. Use it to make the best of any stuation. Be creative, resourceful and loving while you figure out your strengths. Practice the art of forgiveness to allow joy to emerge. Enjoy your time here.

March 15

Sometimes we are living the dream and sometimes too many opportunities coincide, thus overwhelming our once-perfect dream. If you notice this occurring, adopt a lighthearted approach to elevate your wavelength. Mourn if you must. Release. Rise above the turmoil. Meaningful solutions will come from above.

March 16

Expand all the good feelings by finding activities where you can develop and grow on your spiritual path. What have you found so far that works well for you? What do you want to try next?

March 17   ∞

Appreciation and gratitude are powerful thoughts that, through practice, will enhance the alchemy of your heart and your mind. Continue celebrating the blessings that surround you. Write a note to someone you appreciate and admire.

18 March 19

"Don't let yesterday use up   "L'avenir appartient a la gentillesse."
too much of today."   ~ The future belongs to kindness. ~

Cherokee Wisdom   Bertha von Suttner

Soulful Sketchbook

wisdom doodles

Listen, breathe and smile when engaging in a conversation
with someone you want to see again.

Although joy is always shining within you, a little boost is fun.
Create a 'get happy playlist' of your fave songs to help you shine.

Chapter Eleven

March 20   ∞

We are here on Earth to learn how to relate to one another, free from tech. The idea of oneness shows us that if we vibrate at a high enough frequency, we may escape the feeling of human suffering. Intimacy with another being briefly lifts us to this place. We can find it on our own as well. Research 'Oneness Blessing' to explore the practice of elevating your vibrational awareness.

March 21

Wisdom is earned throughout your lifetime, if you are lucky enough to learn as you go. When you were a baby, you did not learn to walk on your first attempt. You kept working on improving yourself until you took your first step. Then, everything changed. Your life today is no different. As you entertain new ideas, you must practice more than once if you wish to see anything change. Take baby steps on mystical paths toward enlightenment and practice until you discover what works so well for you. Share your wisdom so that others may draw upon it for their own guidance.

March 22

Sometimes everything lines up and you may have the pleasure of experiencing great admiration from your peers. Be careful, thoughtful and gracious. If your head inflates, you may lose touch with your heart. Remain aware of the awesome power of being a celebrated, heart-centric leader and you will likely magnetize even more miracles.

March 23

We desire harmony, but settle for much less. We misuse our energy, spending time collecting things and people. Liberate yourself from the idea that you need any thing or anyone to experience harmony.

March 24

When you reach confusion, it is a call for clarity. Sit quietly, focus on your breath, meditate, pray and allow answers to come to you.

25 March 26

"Our greatest glory is not in never falling, but in rising every time we fall."

"Each morning, we are born again. What we do today is what matters most."

 Confucius   Buddha

Soulful Sketchbook

wisdom doodles

Carry out a random act of kindness
with no expectation of reward.

Take simple steps to strengthen your emotional, mental and
physical core. Close your eyes, breathe and discover anew.

wisdom journal

Chapter Twelve

March 27   ∞

From time to time, someone new may enter your life and you feel a sudden rush of energy. You may notice that you can't stop smiling, your heart skipping a beat, your body buzzing, your mind wandering into bliss. Enjoy this gift, for this surge has elevated you to a higher wavelength without you having to do anything! Keep yourself connected to this refreshing insight by being grateful for it, without attaching any feelings of wanting more.

March 28

As a custodian of your community, you must find the courage to develop your greatest strengths, so that you may show up as your own knight in shining armor. What a blessing it would be for all of us to see you grow into greatness. What steps can you take today?

March 29

Conflict resolution is a wonderful skill that may come naturally for you, but if you notice you often feel unhappy, there is a way through it. Forgiveness has the power to transform any conflict. Open the flood gates to forgiveness and harmony may once again be shown to you. Who can you forgive? Who would you ask to forgive you?

March 30

You are valuable to everyone around you. Accept good fortune when it finds you, graciously and say 'thank you, more please.'

March 31

While pursuing worldly endeavors, make time to quiet your mind. Invite the awareness of your breath to the forefront of understanding. Do not let your courageous strides upon terra firma interfere with your willingness to receive miracles, as they are meant for you. Be open. Stay open.

01 April 02

"Life is either a daring adventure
or nothing at all."

"Be the flower that gives
its fragrance to even the
hand that crushes it."

Helen Keller   Imam Ali

Soulful Sketchbook

Practice a proper apology whenever necessary:
Acknowledge your role. Recognize the impact.
Apologize. Ask what you can do to make it right.

Honor and celebrate your greatest moments where you
were courageous enough to make bold moves.

Chapter Thirteen

April 03

At times you may find yourself feeling trapped in a storm of negative, racing thoughts. If you feel like you can't breathe, stop whatever you're doing. Focus on your breath. Soften your heart. Find something, anything to be grateful for. Let love flow out of you with each breath and look for a rainbow after the storm. If you cannot find it, imagine yourself surrounded by beautiful, healing light and allow healing to come to you. Ask for help until you find what works well for you, so that you may help yourself.

April 04

Reflect upon the light within you, so that you may shine upon everyone around you. Illuminate until you feel so happy, the light contained within has no choice but to surge through you.

April 05   ∞

The sun is always shining, as are you. In moments where you cannot see the light, know it is there. Even though the present moment is all we have, it is exciting to peek into the future. You can create a compelling future by projecting your brightest light ahead in the distance to set yourself on the path to a bright, beautiful future.

April 06   ∞

When you are feeling creative, bundle your dreams into one mighty beam of energy so that it may manifest into something greater than you could ever imagine. The sky was never the limit! Practice opening and aligning your chakras to transform your body into a conduit for love, light, magic and miracles. Download a Divine update to your mystic motherboard. Reboot, activate or integrate a new operating system if you wish.

April 07

When interacting with others, we can offer tough love or simply love. A soft, gentle heart will lead to discoveries of happiness and joy.

08 April 09

"Use any excuse to feel good and see what happens."

"Only from the heart can you touch the sky."

Abraham Hicks

Rumi

Soulful Sketchbook

wisdom doodles

Fill your bathtub with bubbles and your heart with love.

With whom can you share your happiness? Pick a friend and mail a handwritten note of gratitude and thanks, just because.

wisdom journal

Chapter Fourteen

April 10

As we dance upon the Earth, we find that life is sweet at times, bitter on occasion and bitter-sweet when we learn from our mistakes. When all is well, we may not think about why. When things are out of balance, we are forced to look. As you look within, imagine your emotions as the ingredients in a Divine dish. A good blend will yield good results. What can you do to add some good into your day?

April 11

Take a nice deep breath. Invite love and light to come to you. Let go of all doubt. Allow it to melt away in this moment. This is an important step to become a conduit for love and light. Your greatest power lies in the way you choose to apply your knowledge and wisdom. When you know better, you do better. Spend the day as a conductor of kindness.

April 12   ∞

Your sensitivity and capacity to love is a blessing. Even though it may feel tough at times, resist the urge to close your heart. Practice developing your emotional strength. Be generous when offering your gifts to others, but be sure your chakras are open.

April 13

One of your greatest gifts is your ability to recognize opportunities where love and kindness is needed most. Be grateful to the people around you. Enjoy the wonderful gifts in your life. Where can you give love and to whom?

April 14   ∞

You are capable of allowing source energy to flow through you. Invite the light to come to you, free from doubt. When it arrives, direct the light through you to anyone you wish. Step into the light. The only way to do it wrong is to not do it at all.

15 April 16

"Be kind to the land. Each day she gives you everything you need."

"The smallest act of kindness is worth more than the grandest intention."

Tibetan Wisdom

Oscar Wilde

Soulful Sketchbook

Treat your mother, or someone else's, to dinner.

Who are your favorite teachers and why?
What could you do to honor them throughout your life?

Chapter Fifteen

April 17

Occasionally, you may notice you are nearing a breaking point. Be honest with yourself, trust yourself and slow your pace to continue making measured progress toward your current goals. This will strengthen the foundation to help prepare for what may come.

April 18

Like the tide, our emotions and our entire experience on Earth follow patterns and cycles. Sometimes we feel great pain and other times, great fortune and prosperity. From a Buddhist perspective, the idea of Karma refers to action, with intention that has consequences in future life cycles. From a mystical perspective, the Universe always supports you, if you allow it. Take a thoughtful and caring approach.

April 19   ∞

For a Divine power boost, recharge your heart and soul in the grace of a rising or setting sun. As you continue to bloom and grow, explore your community to connect with others who may be on a similar path.

April 20

We are often so hard on our self. Take an honest look into your eyes. Have compassion for yourself. Give yourself some of that wonderful love you are giving everyone else. Forgive yourself for any areas where you may have forgotten to take care. May peace be with you. Go thoughtfully into your day with a mind full of love.

April 21   ∞

One of the great challenges when learning how to master your sensitivity is discovering emotional stability. As you enhance your gifts, you will see them as powerful ways to contribute.

22 April 23

"Beware the barrenness
of a busy life."

"Truth is powerful
and it prevails."

Socrates

Sojourner Truth

Soulful Sketchbook

Do not let a word left unspoken keep you from your greatest song.

Take a 24-hour truth challenge. Be honest with yourself and anyone you encounter for the next 24 hours. Take notes.

Chapter Sixteen

April 24

As you sit peacefully, allow meaningful questions to arise within. How can you best spend the time you have today? How can you be of service? Where can you help? Who can you help? Start with you and expand in all directions.

April 25   ∞

We all make mistakes. We don't always try to fix them. Restore harmony by having the integrity and courage to make amends. If you observe injustice, intervene where you feel you must and above all, seek peace. What are your core values and guiding principles? Refine everything from a higher place.

April 26

One of your greatest assests is your ability to bring love to the table. Your loving heart, finely tuned intellect and great wisdom can lead to heroic acts of diplomacy and professionalism. Skip the war.

April 27   ∞

Throughout life, it is important to assess and decide what is working well and what isn't. Keep the good, leave the rest. As you take your next steps, remember that you are a lightworker. Light the way.

April 28

Fear drives us away, while aspirations may move us forward. Regardless of how you got here, you may find yourself feeling stuck, juggling a bit more than you can handle. Even in serious cases, a lighter approach may relieve some of the pressure. Surf the waves to ease their impact upon you.

29 April 30

"Nam Myoho Renge Kyo."   "To get lost is to learn the way."

Buddhist Mantra   African Proverb

Soulful Sketchbook

wisdom doodles

Join a group; find a place where you can be part of something positive
and empowering; a place where you can contribute.

Research gracious and heroic leaders of today as well as
throughout history and write them thank you notes.

wisdom journal

Chapter Seventeen

May 01   ∞

In stillness and silence, allow racing thoughts to calm. Allow deep, relaxing breath to bring you closer to peace. Ask for guidance. Whatever you believe in, it only matters that you call for guidance, not what you call it. As you explore your conscious mind, allow your unconscious mind to cross into this moment. Let answers flow through you so they may manifest miraculously to you from above.

May 02

Even when clouds appear, the sun is always shining. Today is a day to be as joyful as the sunflower, filled with wonder. Your task is to supercharge yourself and empower others. A pure beam of sunlight rests within you and thus, you are always shining.

May 03   ∞

Part of the human experience includes a dance with the devil. It is not real. The practice of awareness of your authentic self will lift you from the shackles of the mind which seek to diminish you. If you notice you are sabotaging your own efforts, it is likely the ego recognizing it may be lost in this moment. Expand your heart through compassion to give way to the truthful expression of the angelic possibilities within you. Release your fears and ask for help.

May 04

Your love and light is a reflection of your sensitivity. Immense wisdom may be difficult to see at times, but is always available. Disconnect from tech. Walk under the stars. Touch the trees. Howl at the moon.

May 05

So many dreams, some may call you foolish. No need to listen to them. Take a moment, think about what you want and need. Listen to your heart. A cosmic leap will bridge the gap to a dream come true.

06 May 07

"When all the trees have been cut down;
when all the animals have been hunted;
when all the waters are polluted;
when all the air is unsafe to breathe;
Only then will you discover
you cannot eat money."

Cree Prophecy

"Remember that not getting
what you want is sometimes
a wonderful stroke of luck."

Dalai Lama

Soulful Sketchbook

When you see a terrible story on the news, invent ways to help
the people in need. Thoughts and prayers are a powerful start.

Place your bare feet into the Earth and breathe for a simple way
to recharge your body, mind and spirit. What else can you do?

wisdom journal

Chapter Eighteen

May 08

In moments when your heart is open, tears of joy may spring from deep within your soul. This swell of inspiration will instinctively move you to care for yourself and others. Carry this energy with you throughout the day. One of the most attractive qualities to humans is one who is able to take care of him/her/them self. How can you reach a state of excellence?

May 09

It is wise to keep your mind so clear that you may leap to higher frequencies. Acknowledge and release any thoughts rooted in fear that may be holding you down. An open mind will keep the heart open. An open heart heals the world. Release anything you are holding on to. Be charitable and the Universe will respond in kind.

May 10

Development of self-esteem can be easy and fun. You can choose to be happy because happiness is your choice. Hold yourself in high esteem, immune from egoic ideas of grandeur. Pick something to celebrate, revel in the joy of the moment and cherish your graceful heart. Let chai tea and tai chi show you the flow from which you may discover ethereal frequencies.

May 11

Habits of wellness will fortify a foundation that will serve you on your path ahead. Appreciate this moment of security as you strengthen your infrastructure of peaceful relationships. As you flow about your day, harmony is simply Divine.

May 12

Time to check yourself out by checking in with yourself. Put your face close to the mirror (not a selfie cam), look into your eyes and give yourself some love. A moment of self-reflection goes a long way. Behold the awe-inspiring lover of life looking back at you! Remember to smile into those beautiful eyes staring back at you.

13 May 14

"You become what you believe."   "If a person can do it, I can do it."

Oprah Winfrey Geena Davis

Soulful Sketchbook

wisdom doodles

To anyone who feels anything other than
beautiful, appreciated, strong, intelligent and cherished,
perhaps you are in a league of your own.

Who inspires you and why?
How can you inspire others?

wisdom journal

Chapter Nineteen

May 15

The wisdom of the many days you have lived contain the light to lift you up. Pay close attention to your dreams. Left unspoken, they may never have the chance to grow. You can empower yourself by writing down your dreams and sharing them. Breathe them into your heart. Give them room to expand. This measured approach will lay the foundation to guide you. Imagine your bright world and build it.

May 16

As you learn to notice the patterns that are in constant flow all around you, you can develop a practice of preparation and enjoyment. When fortune favors you, enjoy it. When it appears as though your luck has taken a turn, it is a reminder to prepare. You can easily recharge yourself daily at sunrise or sunset. Take a walk and bask in the glow and glory of the gentle sunlight as it moves along its orbit. You don't have to understand it all, but you can learn to make the best of any situation. Trust that fortune favors you.

May 17

Engage in a community of loving, open-minded people. Find mentors to guide you. Spiritual strength unifies our heart with our soul. Develop your faith to deepen it. It matters not what you call it, only that it be done. Practice forgiveness. Practice faith.

May 18

When you take on too many tasks, each task suffers along with everyone involved. Stop. Breathe. Step back. Refocus with a lighter, child-like approach and you may be lifted. Dance.

May 19

One key quality of a trusted leader is to be an artisan of emotions. As you learn and grow, keep your heart and mind open to all the wonder that awaits you in this world. Close your eyes, breathe in compassion and exhale gratitude. Repeat.

20 May 21

"There can be no peace without understanding."

"It is beautiful to be forgiven, but in order to be forgiven one must first forgive."

Senegalese Proverb

Pope Francis

Soulful Sketchbook

wisdom doodles

In matters of mistake, judge not by what one has done,
but what has been learned. Forgive yourself.

Is there anyone you wish to make amends with? Even in their
absence, you can imagine it. Say 'I forgive you, please forgive me.'

wisdom journal

Chapter Twenty

May 22

When you are facing decisions that feel of the utmost importance, seek counsel from your trusted advisors. Be willing to learn from your life experiences. As you grow into a wise elder, you may become a trusted advisor. Wield your power by practicing diplomacy. A wise diplomat understands the strength of her song.

May 23

Your thoughts come and go, often so fast, they may keep you awake at night. You have the ability and choice to stop this. Choose thoughts that lift you higher. Focus your attention on something you can feel grateful for. Focus on your breath. Breathe. Allow yourself to slow down. Focus on the positive and empowering aspects of who you are and allow that to expand. Practice the artistry of allowing gratitude.

May 24   ∞

There is a force within us that burns as bright as the sun. Through consistent meditation, we feel lifted and lighter, thus enabling the potential for physiological improvements. By connecting with this part of our self, we break free from any ideas that seek to bring us down. We are lifted to a level where we feel light, bright and beaming. As you look ahead, be gentle and use your power for good.

May 25

Strength and power, when presented with grace and charisma, is attractive and beautiful. Lead with Light for a day of miracles.

May 26

Take time to recharge your gentle heart. Stay grounded in grace as you look to the heavens for guidance with big decisions. Approach with love and your light touch will be appreciated and celebrated.

27 May 28

"Gratitude is the sign of noble souls."   "If you can't live longer, live deeper."

Aesop   Italian Proverb

Soulful Sketchbook

wisdom doodles

Give thanks and/or five dollars to the next person you witness
doing something out of the kindness of their heart.

Who can you be thankful for?
What can you be thankful for?

wisdom journal

Chapter Twenty-One

May 29

As you know, no thing lasts forever. Even though your love will remain, it may be time to move on. Focus on the lessons you have learned. Where have you grown? Where could you go from here? Ground yourself in gratitude and appreciate the journey that brought you here thus far. Look ahead to a bright future and it may be. Your willingness to begin and flexibility along the way could be most helpful.

May 30

If you are feeling heightened sensitivity, it is a call to action as a new phase of life begins. What lessons and wisdom do you bring to the table? Not sure? Use your tools, experience and talents to figure it out. Act. Trust your intuition as you step gracefully through this beautiful day.

May 31

Take a moment to reflect upon your life, your wisdom and the light within you. Where can you shine your brightest? What are your greatest gifts and how can you share them with others? If you sense any blocks, acknowledge them so that you may release them. Only then will the light shine through. Order your day sunny side up.

June 01

If you feel trapped or unhappy, it is a call to action. Release fears, doubt and worry, for these feelings no longer serve you. Focus your time and attention on what matters most to you. You get to decide what that means. If you do not know where to begin, start with gratitude. As you greet the rising sun, glide gently with grace upon your day. Hold yourself accountable to be in joy.

June 02

Approach today with light. Be playful. Think about what you could learn and how you could use it. Explore and be willing to bend.

03 June 04

"You exist in time,
but you belong to eternity."

"True knowledge exists in knowing
that you know nothing."

Bhagwan Shree Rajneesh

Socrates

Soulful Sketchbook

wisdom doodles

Donate money when you can. Donate time when you can't.

Flexibility can strengthen you enough so that you bend, instead of break. To which situations can you apply this idea?

wisdom journal

Chapter Twenty-Two

June 05

We get in life what we focus on. When things are going well, we want it to last forever. However, if the harmony you seek becomes elusive, remember you have the power to find your path home in any given moment. Even if it seems like you feel trapped in a bad dream, your future rests within you. Click your heels thrice. Ask. Believe. Receive.

June 06

Ambition will eventually lead to a breaking point where you can handle no more. Balance is essential for your strength. When you take on more than you can handle, you have a few options. Reduce or delay some endeavors or continue full steam ahead, with help. Be kind and loving to all who help. Kindness will create a marvelous foundation for you to build upon. Love with all your might.

June 07

You bring excitement and passion to the world around. Your cool head brings a most excellent balance to your fiery heart. As you embark upon this epic day, let your illustrious sense of adventure lead you through it.

June 08

When you notice a cycle ending, it is time to release all attachment to enable total freedom from it. Transformation can be messy, but deep breath will allow for peaceful transitions.

June 09

As a new phase begins, ask for miracles to come to you. Then remember to remain open to receiving them. Call it luck, Karma, prayers or blessings. Regardless of label, good fortune favors you. Gratitude will magnify the wonders that await you.

10 June 11

"We make a living by what we get, but we make a life by what we give."

"When you show the moon to a child, it sees only your finger."

Norman MacEwen

Zambian Proverb

Soulful Sketchbook

wisdom doodles

When teaching a child, let them teach you.

What have been some of the greatest moments of your life?
Who was with you along the way?

wisdom journal

Chapter Twenty-Three

June 12

Kindness and compassion, toward yourself and others, are among the greatest tools in your toolbox. You may live your entire life and never know your true value in this world. When faced with challenges, connect with your heart, even if it feels broken. Gently allow yourself the strength to create a foundation from which to rise.

June 13

When conflict arises, remain engaged through a commitment to peace. Solutions are possible, but only when everyone is willing to peacefully listen to each point of view. Clarity may come if you acknowledge any feelings of fear and release them one by one.

June 14

Your tender heart is a gift that sometimes includes the weight of the world. Your intuitive nature is the keystone to your powerful family bonds and your loving friendships. Empathy is the miracle of your heart. Learning to care for yourself sets the tone for great leadership. Lead by example. When you dive into yourself, tread lightly.

June 15 ∞

Ambition often leads to a crossroads and here we are again. Meditate first, then speak. You may need to step up and stand up or step back and stand down. Communication and compromise will strengthen all bonds of partnership. Open your eyes wider, then add more light.

June 16

Our elders possess wisdom we cannot yet imagine. They are kings and queens among us. Navigating a lifetime of joy, wounds, mistakes and triumph brings great wisdom. They are to be experienced, not forgotten. Listen, with love. What can you do to show your elders how much you appreciate them?

17 June 18

"If the highest aim of the captain was to preserve his ship, he would leave it in port forever."

"Let light shine out of darkness."

Thomas Aquines

2 Corinthians 4:6

Soulful Sketchbook

wisdom doodles

If you see an emergency, respond. Call 9-1-1. Instead of filming it,
help the people in front of you. Take the opportunity to finely tune your
sense of moral obligation by asking yourself, "How can I help?"

Who are your role models?
What about them do you admire the most?

_____

_____

_____

_____

_____

_____

wisdom journal

Chapter Twenty-Four

June 19   ∞

When your heart is overflowing with love, you may find yourself so overwhelmed with joy, you naturally begin singing and dancing. What a sight to behold! Discover and develop healthy ways to intensify and enhance your love of life. Stay current with the current and a fountain of youth may spring from within.

June 20

Sometimes the message is simple. Believe in yourself so strongly, all other thoughts vanish from the ether of possibility. You got this.

June 21

Everything in our Universe is in sync with a cycle we are only beginning to understand. Look to the light above - the starlight, the moonlight and the sunlight. Look to the light within - the light of your heart shining through your eyes and smile. Allow the light to guide you forward through any situation. The light is the Truth.

June 22   ∞

Harmony exists to show us heaven on Earth. In music, harmony is created when musical notes are in agreement. In life, you can create harmony through a happy, peaceful flow of Love. If you notice parts of your life drifting away from what you desire, develop a daily practice of intentionally asking for miracles to find your open heart. Harmonize each part of your life and savor the heavenly fruit.

June 23

Part of the magic of life is allowing miracles to flow through you. A seed planted does not show you what it is capable of. First, you must trust. Then, add love and light. With proper care, you shall witness the miraculous expression of magic that exists within every seed. In these moments, let nothing cloud your vision. Stand in awe and stay there.

24 June 25

"A good idea is meaningless without the courage to act."

"Bravery never goes out of fashion."

Alexander Maggio   William Makepeace Thackeray

Soulful Sketchbook

wisdom doodles

Courage can be found atop the tallest mountains
and upon the calmest sea.

If you were a superhero, what superpowers would you have?
What are your greatest strengths?

wisdom journal

Chapter Twenty-Five

June 26 ∞

When you feel as though you may need some space, it can be quite valuable to step back and look at the situation from other points of view. Review each perspective objectively, as though you are a Divine detective. When your vision expands, what comes to light? Take responsibility for your role. Practice being a peace officer.

June 27 ∞

The path to enlightenment is a twisted web of wonder and worry and learning to let go of it all. Sometimes we feel the weight of the world and sometimes we feel as though we hold the keys to the Universe. Ride the waves as they come. Enjoy the feeling of wholeness that comes as you learn to elevate yourself. One day, you may find a path of enlightenment. Research spirit animals and animal totems and enjoy divine gifts as they are delivered to you.

June 28 ∞

Even when things seem out of order or chaotic, things are in order. Ground yourself. Put your bare feet into the sand, the dirt, into Mother Earth. Upload ancient wisdom. Find a way to be at peace even amid the perception of chaos. Touch the trees.

June 29

Take great care of yourself and those around you as you always do. Attract great love by giving the best of yourself. If you falter, reset yourself through prayer, meditation, gratitude and grace.

June 30 ∞

As a disciple of love and light, the Universe can work through you, as you allow. Ask your angels to lead the way. Inspire a miraculous, marvelous connection with the hearts and minds of everyone you meet. Diplomacy will always foster the creativity required for peace. As you walk upon the Earth, take every opportunity to spread your wings to enjoy adventures filled with whimsy and wonder.

01 July 02

"No act of kindness, no matter how small, is ever waster."

"The friends of our friends are our friends."

Aesop

Congolese Proverb

Soulful Sketchbook

Ask the Universe to place you in your highest and
best use today. Be the answer to someone's prayer.

With your creativity, ingenuity and gratitude, what can you
do to be an angel for your family, friends, neighbors, strangers?

Chapter Twenty-Six

July 03

When you make a wish, you open your heart to infinite possibilities. Stay open. Stay mindful. Stay soulful. Stay kind. Who do you wish to be in this moment?

July 04   ∞

We are part of a constant flow of mystical cycles, many that we will never become aware of, let alone understand. Taking a break is a healthy way to evaluate your life. Sometimes we must simply stop and think. Allow yourself to let go of what no longer serves you. No need to worry. As one cycle ends, a new one begins. Trust Up.

July 05   ∞

When things seem to be moving at the speed of light, gain greater perspective by lifting yourself to a higher wavelength. Everything follows a pattern. Educate yourself and minimize stress by learning how to recognize patterns. Teach yourself to be a mystical princess or prince. Use your intuition and your intellect and see what emerges. Notice the patterns of humanity and your part within it, as a member of it.

July 06

Birth and death are part of the cosmic cycle that allowed us to come here to explore and enjoy Earth. Throughout life, sometimes the healthiest thing you can do is to learn to let go and actually let go. By releasing attachment to that which no longer serves you, you empower yourself to the beauty of new seasons of life.

July 07

The Universe holds everything you want and need. Trust that when you are ready, what you need will be provided. Sometimes there is a time delay and sometimes our wishes are granted quickly. Think about everything you are grateful for. Think about what you want and why. When abundance arrives, remember to enjoy it.

08 July 09

"The wound is the place
where the light enters you."

"I am sorry. Please forgive me.
Thank you. I love you."

Rumi   Ho'oponopono Mantra

64

Soulful Sketchbook

wisdom doodles

Meditation, like bathing, should be practiced daily
for a truly cleansing experience.

A good cry is one way to let your spirit shine. What other
ways could you connect with your soul and let yourself shine?

wisdom journal

Chapter Twenty-Seven

July 10   ∞

If you find yourself stuck between a rock and a hard place, stop looking left and right. Look up! Go higher. Look within. Raise your vibration. Life on Earth can feel tricky at times. The Universe is always ready to give you a helping hand. Connect with the Flow and allow it to lift you higher, even if you aren't stuck. In a jam? Make jelly.

July 11

Tranquility exists under the moonlight, upon the sea, deep in the forest and in learning how to be grateful and how to stay grateful. These are the keys to a beautiful life. Although you may not have what you want, you can always choose to find the silver lining.

July 12   ∞

Mental overload may lead to darkness. Stop, breathe, disconnect. Look within while you ask for miracles. Mindfulness will lead you into the place where the light within may emerge. What can you do to be the change that you wish to see?

July 13

When the path forward is unclear, light the way with your passion and ability to focus. Act with care and thought. A journey may be imminent before a new path is shown to you. What solutions can you imagine as you take your next steps? Dream Up.

July 14

Your skills, talent and hard work may lead to recognition by your peers. When this occurs, remember that you most likely did not reach this moment on your own. Honor the mighty companions who have helped along the way. How can you recognize and acknowledge those who may have helped you on this path?

15 July 16

"If you have a garden and a library, you have everything you need."

"Hold a true friend with both hands."

Cicero African Proverb

Soulful Sketchbook

wisdom doodles

May any storm within pass as gently as the autumn breeze.

Tranquility follows sorrow. It can also be part of
your deliberate creation. What makes you Zen?

wisdom journal

Chapter Twenty-Eight

July 17

Lower wavelengths lend themselves to injustice, pain and suffering. If things look bleak, ground yourself in gratitude and look again. Speak only words of love. Thoughts of light will strengthen you. Have faith that peace is possible. Allow yourself to be lifted into a higher mind. Restore justice by speaking truth to power, when you must.

July 18   ∞

Holding on to pain can sometimes lead to suffering. Take a deep breath. Have faith in Divine expressions of love, for it is how you were created. Activate mystical power through prayer, meditation or another light-healing modality. Say 'I allow, I am willing, I release.' Hippocrates said, "The natural healing force within each of us is the greatest force in getting well." Explore healthy ways to release your pain. It begins with your willingness to acknowledge any pain so that it may be released. Healthy self can be re-written as heal thyself. Could any part of your story be re-written?

July 19

As you wake each morning, gently breathe in thoughts of love to light the path ahead. This union of your heart and mind gives you the foundation for a beautiful day. Imagine peace and prosperity and they will have no choice but to flow through you and thus, to you. Your spiritual wealth is the result of several days well lived.

July 20   ♥

Acts of grace will hold all who bear witness in captivating enchantments. Walk with kindness upon this Earth and the Earthlings will thus be magnetized to you and hypnotized by you. Allow yourself to radiate love and light and you shall attract love and light. How can you glow, shimmer & shine even brighter upon those around you?

July 21

A gracious leader develops the strength to balance diplomacy and force. Strength lies not with a cache of weapons. Look up and look within for a soulful stream of wisdom.

22 July 23

"Nearly all men can stand adversity, but if you want to test a man's character, give him power."

"It is the mark of an educated mind to be able to entertain a thought without accepting it."

Abraham Lincoln

Aristotle

Soulful Sketchbook

wisdom doodles

Democracy is dependent on your participation. Register to vote, research candidates and vote in elections. If you feel "We the People" is not being handled justly, may I suggest 'All Hands on Deck.'

If you could teach something amazing you have learned, what would you say and to whom?

wisdom journal

Chapter Twenty-Nine

July 24   ∞

Life can leave us a little rough around the edges, at times. When you notice a desire for some refinement, dance naked in the moonlight. Bathe in the magnificent glow, reflect upon your day, harmonize with nature and connect with the flow to find the fountain of youth. This can be achieved literally or creatively through metaphor.

July 25

Even the brightest light casts a soft shadow. In the softest shadow rests a tender heart. In moments of eclipse, let the light shine while you stay open to miracles. The light within is a Divine loan from source energy. When magnified, it can cause quite the spectacle, capturing the attention of our fellow sunbeams. The tender hearts all around will reward you with admiration, appreciation and love. Enjoy it deeply.

July 26

When your best self is obscured by your immature, untrained self, you may find your self in a tough spot. In other words, when you fall on your face, get up. Brush yourself off. Ask yourself what the lesson is and take a step forward with an open heart.

July 27

You are on one amazing journey, surrounded by beautiful souls. When the angles of light are just right, angels emerge. When any opportunity for adventure finds you, say yes!

July 28

Youth is freedom from care. When we act carefree, life is beautiful. When we act careless, life is insane. We cannot take responsibility for our choices until we grow and learn the distinction. Honor and pride await those with the courage to care. How can you be even more mindful and thoughtful?

29 July 30

"He who lives in harmony
with himself, lives in
harmony with the universe.

"Educating the mind
without educating the heart
is no education at all."

Marcus Aurelius   Aristotle

70

Soulful Sketchbook

wisdom doodles

When observing childish behavior, teach the compassionate way.

What were some of your favorite things to do as a child?
What can you do now to spark that child-like wonder?

wisdom journal

Chapter Thirty

July 31

Your open mind and open heart will keep you light as a feather. If you notice you have fallen into some low-level energy, raise your vibration to expand your vision. Carve a path of light in front of you. Get your bare feet into the Earth. Allow the sun, the moon and the stars to recharge your soul. Thoughts based in fear rob us of you. We all need you to go deeper and fly higher.

August 01

Many believe we are 'spiritual beings having a human experience.' Whatever you decide, believe or come to know, all is well. You may connect with the wonderful gifts of our Universe through prayer, meditation, music, art, dance, athletics or anything else that opens your heart. As you connect, you will supercharge your human into a being of love and light. Love Up.

August 02   ∞

As you explore the wide whirled intertwined web of humanity, center yourself in your heart and soul. Elevate your wavelength so high, that you clearly see the patterns that we all follow as we walk upon the Earth. If you can finely tune your sensitivity high enough, it will be as if x-ray vision is one of your superpowers. Rise Up.

August 03

Ambition is exciting at first then can quickly diminish if it causes other areas of your life to fall out of balance. If you notice this occurring, evaluate your priorities and your abundance and start anew. Replace ambition with gratitude, then begin to build.

August 04

Cloudy with storms. Sunny and crystal clear. Our thoughts mimic the weather and you can forecast the light. When you notice clouds catching the light, ask that the truth be brought forward. Release, cry, let it rain, so that the sun may shine through. As the storm passes, a spectrum of color appears from the clear light and you are left only with gratitude and grace. Become the rainbow after any storm.

05 August 06

"The future depends on what we do in the present."

"Om Mani Padme Hum."

Mahatma Gandhi

Sanskrit Mantra

Soulful Sketchbook

wisdom doodles

Drink tea instead of coffee, once per week, at least.

If you could tell your 5-year old self how to develop self-esteem and self-worth, what would you say?

_____

_____

_____

_____

_____

_____

wisdom journal

_____

Chapter Thirty-One

August 07

Imagine yourself as an angel, with a wingspan that extends far beyond your body. Let your wings expand and ask that you be lifted to your highest and best use. Imagine yourself in a place where you feel comfortable, secure, peaceful and calm. In this place, explore the depths of your soul to activate ancient wisdom. Practice in your comfort zone, then leave it. Let the sacred spirit, or whatever name you choose, guide you.

August 08

As you dream, you are thus lifted into a bright future. When making the journey, however, you must step carefully and wisely. The edge of a cliff need not force fright upon you. Let faith bridge the gap from where you are today and where you believe you'd like to go.

August 09

There is always room for more love in your life. Expand your shell. Be inclusive. Take every opportunity to work in cooperation with others. Radiate unconditional love for magnetic moments of friendship, intimacy and joy. Unite with your highest self.

August 10

In the bakery of life, we see many recipes that yield many results. Some are beautifully sweet, some terribly bitter and others seem totally rotten. If you notice life seems to be turning bitter for yourself or others, simply add sugar.* This is your reminder to enjoy the sweetness of life and your ability to sweeten the deal. Even in times of trauma, tiny acts of kindness blended with gratitude can yield a beautiful, bitter-sweet moment that becomes a masterpiece of life. *Grace is a suitable substitute for sugar.

August 11

Your sphere of influence expands greater than you may ever know. Protect your creations with an open, loving heart. Be angelic.

12 August 13

"A leader who does not take advice is not a leader."

"If every 8-year old in the world is taught meditation, we will eliminate violence from the world within one generation."

Kenyan Proverb

Dalai Lama

Soulful Sketchbook

Research inspiring and thoughtful people whose powerful voices are still needed. Think about who comes to mind for you and weave their wisdom into your day.

Think about someone you love and imagine nice things you could do for them. Now pick someone you dislike and do the same.

Chapter Thirty-Two

August 14

Have fun now. That's a direct order from above! Make it easy and make it happen. If you find yourself in a funk, it means it may be time to have some fun, k?

August 15

We need not be running around the Earth in chaos, even though our racing thoughts may tell us otherwise. Your willingness to become aware makes it so. From this awareness, you can supercharge your cells to vibrate into the patterns of creation, beyond infinite thought. In knowing nothing, we can begin to know everything. As a conduit for light, you can download and distribute love without any desire for attachment. Beyond all that we think we know is everything else. As above, so below.

August 16

The mystic forcefield through which life is created may appear as 'empty' space, but we know better. Each individual cell has room for life and life itself. To protect what you create, give it room to grow.

August 17

On the spectrum of the human condition, why do we connect with some people and never with others? Wavelengths play a large part in determining our experience on Earth. Like radio waves, one must be in tune with an exact frequency for communication to flow. We operate in a very similar manner, though our frequency does not have to be exact. Our thoughts determine our behavior and both emit frequencies. Mindful and loving thoughts lead you to higher minded choices, thus attracting new people, places and situations or inspiring a new view of your life as it is.

August 18

When you learn to love yourself without conditions, heaven emerges. In moments when you are open to being quiet, peaceful and calm, Divine gifts will eclipse all disbelief. Allow waves of serenity to now wash over you.

19 August 20

"The fool speaks.
The wise man listens."

Develop your intuition through the exploration of the Eight Limbs of Yoga.

Ethiopian Proverb

Yoga Sutras of Patanjali

Soulful Sketchbook

On a new moon, drive away from the city lights
and see what the world really has to offer.

What would you like to refine about your life right now?
What are the first steps to make it happen?

Chapter Thirty-Three

August 21   ∞

The reality we experience on Earth is real, but not Real. Just as gravity keeps us from floating away, the ego keeps us from knowing Truth. Hell exists as egoic thought. Heaven is just beyond it. When you find life beyond the ego, you'll be so happy, you'll float away. Begin with the deepest breath.

August 22   ∞

As you get closer to finding the place beyond the ego, it (the ego) recognizes your proximity to Truth which means its impending death. To save itself, the ego kicks into high gear to keep you grounded in madness. If you notice an increase in self-sabotage, you may be getting close. Awareness allows you to move beyond the ego. Om.

August 23

Be playful. Be creative. Consider the possibility that everyone is an angel here to play, explore, create and relate. By re-imagining humanity, it may be easier to celebrate and enjoy life. Learn the difference between excellence and perfection. Open up.

August 24

Plan for success. Build a brilliant team. If blinding fear takes over, laugh at it and step into your plan. Create in concert with the Universe for perfect harmony. Lean on others, gently.

August 25   ∞

Sometimes our creativity takes us places we could never imagine. You may love where you are or it may still leave something to be desired. In any case, developing a practice of consistent meditation will ease any pain and enhance any joy. So, in case you forgot again, here's your reminder to 'Om & Repeat'.

26 August 27

"If you want to go quickly, go alone. If you want to go far, go together."

"Great things are done by a series of small things brought together."

African Proverb   Vincent Van Gogh

Soulful Sketchbook

Be creative in love and love will create beyond your wildest dreams.

The execution and quality of your work are critical components beyond any idea. Which of your amazing ideas is next for you?

Chapter Thirty-Four

August 28

In stillness, the answers may find you. Quiet your mind. Calm those racing thoughts by acknowledging them and releasing them. Breathe. Practice. Patience. Breathe. Practice. Patience. Breathe. Patience is rewarded from that which fills your lungs.

August 29   ∞

As you soar and explore, your wireless connection to the cosmos may strengthen. If you find yourself in need of a little help, imagine the Divine link between you and all else. When you realize you are one with all, you are lifted above your perception of it.

August 30

Ancient wisdom is always available, once you are open to downloading it from the ether of all that is, all that ever was and all that ever will be. Seek guidance from above and from within. Ask the angels to show you clear signs that you can easily understand. Learn to recognize the answers as they are shown to you. Learn to see.

August 31   ∞

When you are able to recognize the people in your life as angels, miracles happen. Lower your walls and let your love runneth over. Send love.

September 01   ∞

While envisioning big ideas, take time to notice the smallest details. While allowing the expansion of miracles throughout your world, stay focused on the idea that you are not separate from any other being of light. If you fracture from source energy, you will remain under glass. Your willingness to embrace the idea of oneness will shatter all perceived barriers.

02 September 03

"I am without form, without limit, beyond space, beyond time, I am in everything, everything in me."

"Doing good to others is not a duty. It is a joy, for it increases your own health and happiness."

Swami Rama Tirtha

Zoroaster

Soulful Sketchbook

If you can't give money to a homeless person,
offer a bottle of water and a loving smile.

What could you do to spark your connection to any one
and to invite a sense of oneness into your open heart?

Chapter Thirty-Five

September 04

If you find yourself imagining new endeavors, take a little time to study yourself. Think about what you are passionate about. Write down everything you think you want. Become a scholar of your ideas and interests and make a list of the first steps toward your goals.

September 05

The sweetness of life is to be enjoyed and celebrated. No matter how much stuff you acquire throughout your life, you will probably always want more. Good fortune may continue to favor you if you keep yourself in the flow of gratitude. Even if it doesn't, at least you'll know what you are grateful for.

September 06

Imagine a world where peace is our natural condition and we all show up blasting each other with love. As young children, this is often our experience. How sweet the world. Now, as you transit other phases of life, allow your sensitivity to expand. Nurture your emotional capacity for love and keep your heart open. Your intuition is a gift to be enjoyed and expanded.

September 07

How beautiful it would be to go a day without judgement. A whole day where love reigns, starting with the way you see yourself. As you let Light shine through you, may you remember how tricky transformation can be. Have faith that darkness can not exist when it is brought to Light.

September 08

Each family is a miraculous constellation of love, thus making you a Divine expression of starlight. Shine bright and watch as others delight in your sparkle. Make time to recharge under the midnight sky. Dance naked in the moonlight.

09 September 10

"What seems to us as bitter trials are often blessings in disguise.

"Nothing real can be threatened. Nothing unreal exists. Herein lies the peace of God."

Oscar Wilde

A Course in Miracles

Soulful Sketchbook

wisdom doodles

Support your community school events in any way they wish.

Who has been the sweetest to you and what can you do to pay it back in appreciation and pay it forward in love?

wisdom journal

Chapter Thirty-Six

September 11

The gifts of the Universe are always available, waiting for you to connect. Appreciation and gratitude will move you closer to peace. Even on the darkest of days, the sun is still shining. Release judgement and the ever-present stream of joy will emerge.

September 12

Be generous with your heart. Your kindness will be appreciated in ways you may never know. In moments when you feel like shutting down, keep your heart open. Your gentle touch is needed. You are valuable.

September 13

Light the way as you glow about your day. If your twinkle is on the fritz, get up and go for a walk, at least. Let no one doubt your commitment to sparkle. Motion sparks emotion so that you may shimmer and shine. All will appreciate your effort.

September 14

As we gently step across the tightrope of life, we must learn to perform great balancing acts with our health, our wealth, our relationships. Don't be too tough on yourself. Forgiveness provides the greatest healing in any situation, thus restoring balance here on Earth. Who can you forgive? Who must you forgive? Here's a secret: you can imagine forgiveness and make it into a prayer and it will be. Forgive yourself.

September 15 ∞

Awakening is possible in any moment, with any situation. Bring your awareness to your breath and focus on holding the space for a moment of mindful meditation. When you align yourself, clarity will be downloaded from the ether that surrounds the mystic orbs of our Universe. Reflect upon the people you appreciate most in your life.

16 September 17

"I am entitled to miracles."

"God is in everything I see because God is in my mind."

A Course in Miracles

A Course in Miracles

Soulful Sketchbook

Drop off goodies for your local firefighters and police officers
and practice random acts of appreciation elsewhere.

Study the chakra system of the human body. Discover where
they are and how to allow energy to flow freely.

Chapter Thirty-Seven

September 18

Spiritual growth brings about a sense of peace you can only find at higher wavelengths. As you develop your daily, weekly or occasional practice, enjoy the moments where you tip-toe gently toward enlightenment. Whenever you're ready, dive in. Your tender heart will be reunited with the love that created it.

September 19   ∞

Every strong foundation has cornerstones grounded in love. Let your heart tender the plans to build the framework for your success. If your enthusiasm wanes or you reach stumbling blocks, you've got the blueprints because you just created them!

September 20

Throughout the day, let your imagination play. Keep expanding every thought and see where it leads. Be playful with child-like wonder. Let the sunlight be your fun light. Give your shadows a break. Chase butterflies or snowflakes. If someone sees you, invite them to join you. Maybe you'll make a new friend for life.

September 21

Do not chase a butterfly off a cliff. But if you do, when you hit rock bottom, pick yourself up and ask what lesson can be learned. As the answers appear, write them down. Drop your shield, make amends if necessary and step forward in love. Peace on Earth starts with peace of mind. Peace of mind starts with a mind at peace.

September 22

Prepare to enjoy the day ahead of you, but first, enjoy this moment and now this one. Tender your heart so that you can remain open to receive abundance from the Universe. You got this. Breathe.

23 September 24

"God grant me the Serenity to accept the things I cannot change, the Courage to change the things I can, and the Wisdom to know the difference."

"To one who has faith, no explanation is necessary. To one without faith, no explanation is possible."

Serenity Prayer

Thomas Aquinas

Soulful Sketchbook

wisdom doodles

Buy or make coloring books with your friends and color with them.

What matters most to you? Whatever you feel most compelled
to change in this world, its yours to change. Do it.

wisdom journal

Chapter Thirty-Eight

September 25   ∞

When you learn to enjoy the healthy parts of life, you can take pleasure in building a strong foundation. Delight in yourself, so that you can create a fortified base of operations. Metaphysically, this would be achieved by aligning your chakras. To start, say 'Om.' Gentle tenderize your soul.

September 26

Gratitude, kindness, forgiveness and grace may right all things perceived to be wrong. Be gentle with yourself. We are often hardest on ourself. What areas of your life can you improve with a more balanced approach?

September 27

Your sensitivity and gentle heart are two of your greatest gifts. As a guardian of our galaxy, you may feel compelled to rescue everyone. Remember to speak from your heart or wait to speak until your heart becomes available again. Being a thoughtful, heart-centered being brings joy to the forefront of your soul, for you are an angel upon Earth. Be kind to yourself.

September 28

Intellect is an exciting aspect of the human mind that will give one pause for thought. As you delve into your mind, seek diplomatic pathways. Lead with a thoughtful, tactful approach. Smile with an open heart, enjoy kindness and be mindful throughout your day.

September 29

Sometimes we nest, sometimes we must fly the coop. It is time to fly. Spread your wings and soar with grace. Share the best of yourself with everyone you meet. You are an angelic force for good. Be fierce, yet centered in soul.

30 September ♥ October 01

"If you risk nothing,   "Joy shared is doubled.
you risk everything,"   Sorrow shared is halved."

Eleanor Roosevelt   Swedish Proverb

Soulful Sketchbook

One voice is enough and shall be strong enough
for you to rise above adversity.

Honor everyone who has treated you with grace and love.
Who has been most caring and gentle with your heart?

Chapter Thirty-Nine

October 02   ∞

We are granted temporary use of a temple for our brief visit to Earth. Our body is a vehicle for the miraculous expression of love and light. From time to time, you may feel the urge to retreat from life. If this occurs for you, choose healthy ways to reconnect with your beautiful self, then get back out there! Mindful breathing and meditation may be a very, very good place to start. What comes to mind for you?

October 03   ∞

Truth will be seen when you find your path to stillness. Clarity is ever-present in the warm glow of sunlight. To activate your direct link to the Universe, be willing to open your mind's eye.

October 04

It's healthy to seek help, but everything you want and need is within you now. Even this guide is simply that, a guide. You must do the work, develop a practice for yourself that brings you peace, comfort and joy and warms your own heart. Every moment, any moment is an opportunity to begin anew. Take a nice, deep breath. Breathe.

October 05

Take any opportunity to help others, with and without recognition. It sends a wave of Love throughout the Universe that inevitably will grow into a tsunami of open hearts. Change your lens, refocus and look again.

October 06

A valuable lesson emerges when you act and react with generosity and kindness - nothing else matters. Tender your own heart and you will gain the power to warm even the coldest of others. Your golden touch makes it so. Take pleasure in a rising tide, for we are all lifted.

07 October 08

"If you want to lift yourself up, lift up someone else."

"Next to excellence is the appreciation of it."

Booker T. Washington   William Makepeace Thackeray

Soulful Sketchbook

Work on a holiday for a parent, whenever possible.

When you find yourself in the presence of someone who feels ice cold, what can you do to melt the ice?

Chapter Forty

October 09

When your hands are full, you have a few options: drop everything, give up, ask for help, push onward. Whatever you choose, remember the dark of night always yields to the spark of light. A moment of surrender provides a bright opportunity for growth.

October 10

You hold the keys to your bright future. Courage and faith will keep you on track. Ask for clear signs and the path shall come to light. Look up, look within. Your emotions are the energetic forces to help you move forward and they are sometimes as volatile as the weather. If you have stalled, regain momentum by expanding your heart. Then choose from the array of potential that exists in any moment.

October 11

Harmony flows within our core. It is our essence and essential to thrive. Remember this even in the most difficult situations. Increase your brightness, nurture yourself and those around you. A pleasant experience is always appreciated. Seek harmony.

October 12

Birth and death are miraculous passageways to and from Earth. Our time here is measured. Enjoy the freedom and pleasure that comes with being human. Life is to be in Joy. Joy, joy, joy!

October 13

Your purpose in life will continually update itself when you quiet your mind and ask for clear signs that you can easily understand. As the world turns, you can dial up the drama or you can bring peace and love. Do you wish to be a prince or princess of darkness or a bringer of light? For it will be as you wish.

14 October 15

"The best time to plant a tree was 20 years ago. The second best time is now."

"In the moment of crisis, the wise build bridges and the foolish build dams."

Chinese Proverb

Nigerian Proverb

Soulful Sketchbook

wisdom doodles

On a full moon, howl like the wolf.
It is a great way to release some stuff.

You have the power to spark wonder in everyone
around you. How can you rise to the occasion?

wisdom journal

Chapter Forty-One

October 16   ∞

Tough times call for tough choices. Rest is a critical component of self-care. As you learn to care for yourself, you can learn to enjoy the value of rest for what it is, a cosmic reboot. Other cultures honor this idea. One who doesn't rest will eventually break. Develop your meditation practice for mental and emotional flexibility.

October 17

Even in moments where all hope seems lost, there is a silver lining to be discovered. Take baby steps. One step at a time. Side step. Step forward. Step backward. Duck and cover. Jump for joy. A step in any direction is merely a movement on the joystick of life. It will move you closer to a lesson to be learned, the silver lining.

October 18

Sometimes even when we try our best, everything is lost. In these moments, may healing find you. May Love fill your heart. May you be and see Light with every glance. May your soul be at peace, today and everyday. May you learn and grow as you carve anew.

October 19   ∞

Chakras are energy centers throughout our body. Our hands have chakras as well. There are limits to what we can hold on to, figuratively and actually. By loosening your grip, your open hands can receive wonderful gifts that may otherwise pass you by.

October 20

Good morning angel. Your wings are ready. It's time to fly. Open your mind, spread your wings and the Universe shall provide a breeze worthy of flight.

21 October 22

"The greatest danger for most of us is not that our aim is too high and we miss it, but it is too low and we reach it."

Michaelangelo

"Life is a mirror: if you frown at it, it frowns back; if you smile, it returns the greeting."

William Makepeace Thackeray

Soulful Sketchbook

wisdom doodles

The lost art of civic engagement should be
applauded and awarded until it is normal again.

You may never know your true value in the lives of others.
How can you aim even higher and expand all the good?

wisdom journal

Chapter Forty-Two

October 23

Program your day with time to soar. Take flight! Enjoy the view from above and the perspective it brings. Even the best of flights must end. Upon landing, take the opportunity to recharge. In moments of darkness, keep your gaze fixed to the horizon. Dawn is near. When the light comes, you shall soar again. Be mindful.

October 24

The world is yours to enjoy. With heightened sensitivity and intuition, you may drift between sensing 'disturbances in the force' and the feeling that 'all is well'. As the waves wash over you, stay grateful for the gift of emotional sensitivity. Take every opportunity to laugh. Out loud. Your song is part of a magnificent symphony.

October 25

Allow miracles to flow freely through you, to fill your life and to manifest as they are meant to expand, well beyond your borders. You have the vision. You have the passion. Let nothing stop you from miraculous expansion. You always have the potential. Tap into it and dance.

October 26   ∞

Animal totems, also known as spirit animals, appear often to signal and guide us. When you are willing to see them, it is a reminder to stoke the fires within yourself for great inspiration. Allow your spirit animals to activate your timbre. Visit a lake, river or ocean to discover the stream within. Who can you elevate today? Where can you harmonize? Develop a rhythm that keeps you in sync.

October 27

As you learn to master matters of the heart, it can be easy to get swept up in the flow. Emotional waves mimic what we see on Earth. More waves are always coming. If you find yourself gasping, it is time learn to swim. Trust in your strength and power and ride the waves as they come. A heart full of grace leaves nothing but love.

28 October 29

"A long life may not be good enough,
but a good life is long enough."

"A good laugh is
sunshine in the house."

Benjamin Franklin

William Makepeace Thackeray

Soulful Sketchbook

Practice wellness, demonstrate wellness, share wellness and be well.

What does wellness mean to you?
What does it look like in your daily life?

Chapter Forty-Three

October 30

When you are faced with challenges, it is up to you to decide what impact it will have in your life. The event itself may have little or no meaning. It is important to remember that whatever we focus on, expands. Our reality can change in an instant if we find a way to change our perspective. Take an honest look at the drama of the day and shift your focus if you notice things aren't going well. Become a master of shift.

October 31   ∞

Until you shift your focus, everything will feel quite challenging, hellish even. Breathe. Practice the art of allowing. Life lessons will continue repeating themselves, until you learn something new. What can you learn today? Shed the veil for a moment of authenticity. Remove the mask to see the truth.

November 01

Supercharge your day with a surge of curiousity, creativity and confidence. As you soar, trust the fire that burns within your heart and soul. Power Up.

November 02

Sometimes we're up. Sometimes we're down. Enjoy the ups, explore the downs and remember, they are both temporary. When you sense yourself feeling attached to stuff or people, let go of the feelings of needing or wanting. The feeling of attachment is where suffering exists. Joy is freedom from attachment. Celebrate each moment.

November 03   ∞

Physical fitness is greatest when paired with emotional and mental fitness. Aim for a trifecta of fitness and be willing to bend. Develop great strength by spending a few minutes each morning spent in quiet meditation, prayer or a few minutes of deep, relaxing breath. Let your sacred gifts be your sanctuary in any situation.

04 November 05

"What you do speaks so loudly that I cannot hear what you say."

"Management is about arranging and telling. Leadership is about nurturing and enhancing."

Ralph Waldo Emerson

Tom Peters

98

Soulful Sketchbook

While you are behind the wheel, drive with so much care that you
let it be your mission to protect human life - yours and everyone else's.

Who are the trustworthy leaders you most admire?
Choose from family, friends, historical figures or from film & TV.

Chapter Forty-Four

November 06

Rise above the trends of the seasons by noticing the patterns of humanity. Awareness of our oneness is heavenly, in deed. If you notice some things in your life are upside down, ground yourself, then look again. Clarity shall come when you are willing to see things from higher perspectives.

November 07

In school, electives are not required. The rest of our life is full of electives. When life lessons appear, we must decide if we are willing to participate. We are all here to learn and grow. Our soul is always ready, but our human may be stuck somewhere else. Have the courage to explore your spirit, intellect and passion. Merge the three and see what could be! Elect leaders who demonstrate diplomacy and inspire you. If you don't like what you see, become what you desire. Live as a leader. Preside with passion.

November 08   ∞

You possess the tools capable of great transformation. Launch yourself into the clarity of a bright, cloudless, indigo sky and enjoy the rush of new ideas that come your way. Align thy chakras for liftoff. Do you. Meditate.

November 09

Your emotions are an indication of your vibration. If your emotional state appears to be wavering, go outside and let the sunlight wash over you for a moment or as long as you can enjoy. Light attracts light just as dark attracts dark. Vibrate higher and you'll make bright new friends.

November 10

Smiling creates a cosmic shift capable of restoring harmony and balance. Smile. Smile now. Smile at everyone who comes within ten feet of you today. And tomorrow. If you don't feel like it, act as if and do it anyway.

11 November 12

"It is only possible to live happily ever after on a moment-to-moment basis."

"We do not inherit the Earth from our Ancestors, we borrow it from our children."

Margaret Wander Bonanno

Native American Wisdom

Soulful Sketchbook

wisdom doodles

Recognize where you need help and ask for it.
Use courage to ask for help and grace to receive it.

Practice a moment of mindfulness. Sit quietly, breathe
and listen to what comes to your heart and your mind.

wisdom journal

11:11

Chapter Forty-Five

November 13

Intimacy activates empathy and compassion, if you can enjoy it without fear. Your willingness to understand the depth of your love will bring you closer together. Maintain your sense of self so as to not get lost in each other. Strengthen your authentic connection through your willingness to be vulnerable and to communicate.

November 14   ∞

Your life is a Divine work of art, a beautiful reflection of soul and pure expression of Light. We are meant to reflect, express and share during our brief visit to Earth. If there was no moon, there would be no reflection of sunlight and no change in tides. Imagine yourself without the ability for self-reflection or unable to navigate your emotions. These are key elements to the human experience to be explored in joy.

November 15

Keep yourself grounded in authenticity when working with others. Chances are, you all want the same thing. Cooperation is an art and sometimes both are messy.

November 16

When in alignment, the human body allows for opulent expression of Love. Listen, breathe and smile as you go about your day. If you find yourself talking more than others, quiet your mind to soften your voice. Count from one to twenty-one then go back to one and repeat. Breathe fresh air into your heart.

November 17

What do you love most about life? If you are struggling to think of the answers, find role models who seem to enjoy their life and borrow from them. The more you explore, the more you'll learn what you like and who you are. Whatever you decide, remember to celebrate life. Celebrate every thing, enjoy any thing, love every one.

18 November 19

"We are, after all,
a mere part of creation."

"Simplicity is the
ultimate sophistication."

Oren R. Lyons, Jr., Native American Chief

Leonardi da Vinci

Soulful Sketchbook

wisdom doodles

Compassion is our greatest opportunity.

Explore everything in nature you can possibly find.
Make a list of places you can visit to connect with nature.

wisdom journal

Chapter Forty-Six

November 20   ∞

Peace upon Earth exists. We have all experienced moments of peace. We are all capable of enjoying it in any moment, cultivating it in any moment and destroying it in any moment. The choice is ours. Being Zen is a feeling that is both empty and full and means you experience a feeling of oneness with the world and everything in it.

November 21

The feeling of oneness leaves you lighter and brighter. Build your life from love and light. Express your creativity from this place of wholeness. Share this version of yourself with others and enjoy the co-operatives that appear. As you elevate yourself, you will attract others who are also vibrating at higher wavelengths. This will set the stage for blessed unions.

November 22

Ask. Believe. Receive. Miracles can come as easily as asking for them, believing they are possible and being willing and open to receive the very miracles for which you have asked.

November 23

Facilitate flow and cultivate harmony. Start with your own deep breath. Be a breath of fresh air as you breathe life into your day.

November 24

The cyclical harmony of the Universe guarantees that with everything that ends, something begins anew. Yield to the rhythm, give thanks and show deep appreciation. Be thoughtful, caring, kind, loving and compassionate - to yourself and to others. Unity will be shown to you through patterns of high-minded thought.

25 November 26

"He who thinks he is leading and has no one following him is only taking a walk."	"To send light into the darkness of men's hearts - such is the duty of the artist."
Malawian Proverb	Robert Schumann

Soulful Sketchbook

Practice sportsmanship on and off the field.

Invent ways to reward those who practice any of the actions
that we all say we want: peace, love, harmony and joy.

Chapter Forty-Seven

November 27

As we move through life, friends will come and friends will go. To send a shockwave of love through an old friends world, mail them a handwritten note about what they meant to you and what you learned from your relationship with them. If you aren't ready for that, simply close your eyes and give thanks for your time with them and send love. Both will satisfy the Karmic balance of the Universe.

November 28

Stop looking for a knight in shining armor. Instead, become one for yourself and show up for someone else. Be majestic.

November 29   ∞

The 'call' is always there. Some hear it. Even fewer answer it. We can connect at any time. As we learn from our experiences here on Earth, remember that even though we are bound as an Earthwalker, our wings are always ready to soar, waiting for us to expand them. We are angelic beings in human bodies, always capable of being angelic or being human. The choice is ours.

November 30

The human experience, also known as life, provides us with many wonderful opportunities. When we allow guidance to come through us, wholeness can then be restored where imperfections were once perceived. As you seek counsel, have faith.

December 01

The cyclical nature of life has a way of bringing back people from our past, either in thought or in reality. Either way, it may be wise to question what lessons are to be learned by these miraculous moments. Become your own best friend.

02 December 03

"There is nothing on this earth more to be prized than true friendship."

"Be kind, for everyone you meet is fighting a hard battle."

Thomas Aquinas

Plato

Soulful Sketchbook

Keep jumper cables in your car and offer them whenever possible.
It's an easy way to be the hero of the day.

Who are the friendliest, warmest, kindest,
lightest, brightest people you know?

wisdom journal

Chapter Forty-Eight

December 04

It is possible to have too much of a good thing. If you are overwhelmed, take a step back, let go of the fringe and reconnect with what you are most drawn to. Examine your awesome life, then re-immerse yourself in it.

December 05

When the Universe hands you everything, reach out and connect with a deep sense of gratitude. It is time to enjoy the wonders of the world. It is time to be a wonder of the world. Travel the world by airplane, library or by grounding oneself into the Earth.

December 06

Educate yourself. It's the key to higher learning. Rise to the occasion. The global consciousness is a fascinating prism of perception. Explore so you may discover what you imagine. Imagine what you may discover!

December 07

If you find yourself locked in battle, drop your weapon. It does nothing more than provide a false sense of security. Your true strength rests within. Let diplomacy lead you to clarity. Prepare for diplomacy with a discipline of slow, mindful, deep breath.

December 08   ∞

You can feel hollow from a place of great pain, which leads to emptiness. You can feel hollow from a place of love, which strengthens your connection to the Divine equation that created you. The blessing is that you get to choose to act from your wounded heart or your open heart. How would you like to proceed?

09 December 10

"All plants are brothers and sisters.
They talk to us and if we listen,
we can hear them."

"My grass is green."

Arapaho

Chris Ian

Soulful Sketchbook

wisdom doodles

Pray and/or meditate on any problem or person
every day for 21 days and see what happens.

Honor those who had enough wisdom, courage and diplomacy
to prevent or resolve conflict and let's all learn from them.

wisdom journal

Chapter Forty-Nine

December 11
Enjoy the miraculous moments today, for they are simply Divine. If something feels out of balance, spend time today thinking heavenly thoughts, for they will keep you linked with the beauty of the world around you.

December 12
Check in with yourself to determine if your orbit is following the path you wish. A little self-reflection goes a long way. Dive deeper into the expansion of your intuition. It may even change your trajectory into new planes of existence. Take a break from all screens and 'like, comment, subscribe and follow' the trees, birds, flowers and bees. See what emerges from your connection to Mother Nature. Her infinite wi-fi forever flows to maintain the delicate balance of life itself.

December 13   ∞
For a well-seasoned life, ground yourself through any emotional winter, so that you will easily find your inspiration for the coming spring. Healthy seeds planted today will be of great value when they are called upon later. Cultivate.

December 14   ♥ ∞
For clarity, take a step back and look with another set of eyes. Choose your path only once you wait and weigh the wisdom of others with your own wisdom. Brutal honesty need not be brutal, when it is authentic. Have the courage to speak truth to power and stand up. Let no more be lost.

December 15
Time to clock out, step back, reset, recharge and rest. Make time for an amazing break with a great date: you. Spend time in quiet mind. Affirm all that is good, so it may expand.

16 December 17

"Health is the greatest gift,
contentment the greatest wealth,
faithfulness the best relationship."

"Listen, or your tongue
will keep you deaf."

Buddha Native American Proverb

Soulful Sketchbook

wisdom doodles

Take advice from others, including this book, for what it's worth.

Think about your health, your wealth, your relationships.
What is good and where can you make improvements?

wisdom journal

Chapter Fifty

December 18

Being an Earthling means we are in a constant stream of overlapping paths following cyclical patterns. We orbit each other all day. Occasionally we reunite, bump into old friends, crash into strangers and so on. Like any vessel, small adjustments will help keep you on track. What plane of existence will you program into your human today?

December 19

Open your eyes, your mind and your heart to the wonder, magic and miracles that surround you. Adopt a gentle approach to effectively open, embrace and capture hearts today. Lean into love.

December 20   ∞

When you lean into something, you magnetize it to you. Bring peace to yourself through a gentle bowing of spirit and an open mind. Sit quietly, focus on your breath. Open your hands, let them rest on your thighs. Turn your palms toward the heavens, close your eyes and open your mind to the miracles that are being held in trust.

December 21   ∞

Connect with nature in as many ways possible. Ground yourself in grass, dirt, sand. If it is too cold, gently touch the trees to download ancient wisdom from within the Earth. Practice 'the grateful eight.' Start the day by thinking about eight things you are grateful for. Go! It can be as easy as you make it.

December 22

Think of being on Earth as winning the lottery. You are lucky to be here. Some winners never collect because they never check their ticket. Every perceived negative moment is an opportunity for transformation, if you choose to see it as such. Life is a gift. Glide gracefully above the constant crush of human failings and see the truth of it all instead. Blast everyone with Love. We would all be so lucky. Shift your focus.

23 December 24

"Love, love, love, that is the
soul of a genius."

"You are never so lost that
your angels cannot find you."

Wolfgang Amadeus Mozart

Jeff Rees Jones

Soulful Sketchbook

wisdom doodles

Civic duty can be as easy as sharing a smile with neighbors
or as tough as volunteering to help your community.

Celebrate the moments where you have been most effective
and felt truly blessed. What are some of your greatest moments?

_____

_____

_____

_____

_____

_____

_____

wisdom journal

Chapter Fifty-One

December 25   ∞

There are no forces greater than forgiveness, compassion and love. By keeping your heart in this 'triangle of tranquility,' you can handle anything. Miracles are available in any moment. You have the strength you seek. Believe.

December 26

As you work through complex decisions, let no grain of wisdom pass by you. Collect worldly wisdom, historical wisdom and angelic wisdom from your top advisors. Be advised, be educated. Make decisions thoughfully. Always remember, an open heart says lead with love. Let the rest go.

December 27

Faith has power beyond belief. If you feel as though you have lost faith, look to the stars and ask forgiveness. Allow your intuition to show you thoughtful, honest ancient wisdom. It will be yours to enjoy. Let yourself shine today as you explore these ideas.

> Forgiveness
> Allow
> Intuition
> Thoughtful
> Honest

December 28

When there is too much going on, it's time to bring in the reigns. Approach everything today with gratitude; it will help you lighten up. Observe the waves setting up in the distance and gracefully surf them as they come. Be playful, curious and open.

December 29   ∞

Forgiveness restores balance, harmony and flow. You can enhance your day by forgiving yourself and others. You hold the brush. You get to choose what to pictures to draw. Illustrate with love and light. The masterpiece is yours to create.

30 December 31

"Guide children toward compassion and empathy so they may always be connected to their spirit and humanity."

"Happiness is a choice..."

Robin Jane

Aeschylus

Soulful Sketchbook

wisdom doodles

Say thank you, even when you might want to say something else.

How do you imagine peace?
What do you stand for?

wisdom journal

Chapter Fifty-Two

January 01

Today is a day for optimism, awakening and renewal. This is also a time to prepare. As one era wanes, a grand, new cycle soon begins. What do you wish to refine so you may be fine? Glow, grow and flow.

January 02

Make your plans. Not because a new year has begun, but because this mystical journey will soon end. It is important to make new plans before your current set of circumstances ends. Although, if you find yourself in a gap, faith will guide you on your first steps on the path ahead. If fear creeps back in, courage will yield forward motion.

January 03

Step with care and thought. Move forward with great discipline. Track your progress in measured increments. Choose thoughts that support and enhance your healthy self.

January 04

Make it easy for yourself to feel good about your progress. Small victories must be celebrated along the way. A reward can simply be a pat on the back and then keep going. Lay more track for your train as you conduct your amazing journey.

January 05

A genie knows the power she possess. Perhaps that is why she is so excited and happy. Reset yourself in a blink and a whole new world of possibilities will appear. New people will magically arrive in your life bringing exciting new opportunities. By resetting yourself often, you keep your mind centered on receiving wonderful gifts. Cross your arms and blink. Your wish commands the ether and so it is.

06 January 07

"We cannot teach people anything; we can only help them discover it within themselves."

"Where a woman rules, streams run uphill."

Galileo Galilei

Ethiopian Proverb

Soulful Sketchbook

wisdom doodles

There are friends to be made all over Earth and of course,
in galaxies far, far away. Explore it all.

What areas of your life could use a little refinement?
Who do you love? What do you love?

wisdom journal

Farewell

January 08

Some relationships feel heavenly, effortless and fun. Others need healing, attention and diplomacy. Enjoy the natural occurring divinity wherever it finds you, as it is truly a blessing. Appreciate the relationships where healing is required. Do the valuable work that must be done. Forgive. Love. Repeat.

January 09

When you feel like a fish out of water, it often means you are about to learn something incredible! Today, simply celebrate and enjoy anything and everything, at any stage of progress. As mentioned earlier, pat yourself on the back, literally. It's an easy way to give yourself some love.

January 10 ∞

Life is to be enjoyed. Life is for love. Sometimes it's easier said than done. Have faith because it's always possible. Even though we are wireless beings, untethered from Source, the Universe is wired for your expanding growth. How you choose to define success will determine how your future unfolds. Your life is a Sacred Circle and is to be treated as such. Create a Sacred Space and fill it with anything that will ignite the wonder brewing within.

Closing this Sacred Circle

Now, take a moment to thank yourself for making the time for this journey, for tomorrow begins anew on page 14.

I thank you as well and acknowledge the strength it takes to look within. Your courage and tender heart are the most suitable traveling companions during your time here on Planet Earth. Activate love to radiate love. Who would you like to become in the next stage of your life? We all need you to be activated, loving and light.

May you have many wonderful moments today and every day, filled with Mighty Companions who act with Gratitude & Grace.

Blessings,

Indigo Sky

Soulful Sketchbook

"At some level, everyone is a fully awakened being."

Alexis Kleyla

Nourish to flourish. Review each drop of wisdom from your journey and see a soulful symphony emerge. Compose. Create. Collaborate.

"Out beyond ideas of wrongdoing and rightdoing there is a field. I'll meet you there..."

Rumi

The Greatest Moments of My Life

Sacred Geometry

"Mathematics is the language
with which God has written the universe."

Galileo Galilei

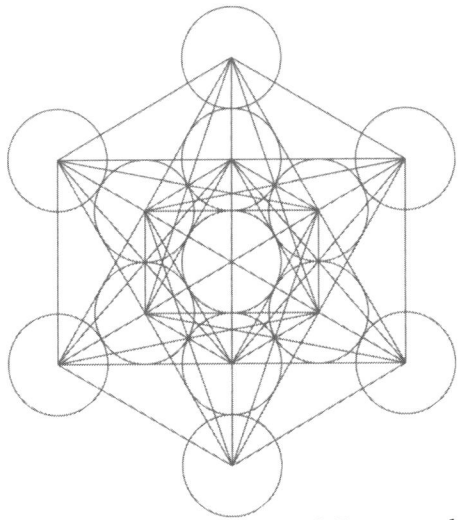

Metatron's Cube

Seed of Life

The pattern that creates life,
and life itself, is all that will ever be.

Evoking the presence of great compassion, let us fill our hearts with our own compassion – towards ourselves and towards all living beings.

Let us pray that all living beings realize that they are all brothers and sisters, all nourished from the same source of life.

Buddhist Prayer

Sending loving thoughts & prayers is an important first step. Please find & invent even more ways to support those in need!

♥ Columbine ♥ Aurora ♥ Manchester ♥ Parkland ♥ Las Vegas ♥
♥ Orlando ♥ Newtown ♥ New York City ♥ San Bernadino ♥

Please visit *NationalCompassionFund.org* to donate money towards helping victims from a specific tragedy.

Honoring people impacted by the massacre in Parkland
Please visit *BrowardEdFoundation.org/StonemanDouglasVictimsFund*
#ParklandStrong #MarchForOurLives

Honoring people impacted by the massacre in Las Vegas
Please visit *LVHealingGarden.vegas*
#PrayForLasVegas #LasVegasStrong

Honoring people impacted by the massacre in Orlando
Please visit *ActLoveGive.org*
#OrlandoStrong #HonorThemWithAction

Honoring people impacted by the massacre in Newtown
Please visit *SandyHookPromise.org*
#SaySomething #SandyHookPromise

Honoring people impacted by the terrorist attacks on 9/11
Please visit *NewYorkSaysThankYou.org*
#LoveIsStronger

Step Forward in Love

Peace on Earth starts with peace of mind.
Peace of mind starts with a mind at peace.

∞

*In a blinding **Spark**, each Life is a Creative Arc*
*It's time to wake up from the **dance** in the dark*
*Anytime anywhere See the **Light** Find the Truth*
*Connect with the **Flow**, find the fountain of Youth*

***Look** around look around at the flowers and trees*
***Look** around look around at the birds and the bees*
*They **know** how to grow, they know how to bloom*
*They live in the **Light**, a place without doom*

*So Give-Up, cease-fire, **stop** listen in Love*
*Look up, **look** within, at the blue sky above*
***Ask** for a miracle and so it is done*
*From the **Source** of Unlimited Light*
*Here comes the **Sun***

***Forgive** don't forget is the secret to living*
*A life **full** with Love, Light and much giving*
***God** is the Artist, your body the brush*
*Your talents' the paint, the **Earth** you can-vas*

Ignite the Sun with your smile
*From the **heavens** above*
*Now take your first **Sacred** breath*
Step Forward in Love

If you can you sing this, share your voice!

@IndigoSkylab #StepForwardinLove

Song Lyrics ©2013

Mighty Companions

Preview of a new book by Indigo Sky

*How to become the **Angel** or **Titan** you were meant to be!*

Excerpt:

Where do we come from? Where are we going? What are we supposed to do while we're here? These are all great questions that have provoked thought through much of human history. What are your thoughts, feelings and beliefs about all of this? There are nearly 7 billion people on Earth and about 4,000 known belief systems. How many are you aware of?

From your darkest days to the greatest moments of your life, you have been given an incredible gift. The gift of your emotional range and the power to move through the symphony of storms that come and go throughout your lifetime. In this guide, we will dive deep into the range of wavelengths that can keep us bound to suffering but can just as easily keep us floating in heavenly bliss.

We will learn to develop our awareness to notice where we are and how our wavelength determines the trajectory of our lives each day. We are always surrounded by mighty companions. We are always capable of being a mighty companion. This new guide aims to lift us all higher, together.

**May *joy* fill your *soul*. May *love* fill your *heart*.
May you be *lifted*, today and every day.**

Mindful Adventures

Pick 3 dates at random and see what messages await.
Change your approach and let a whole new journey emerge!

You may not always be able to control a typo,
but you can control how it impacts your day.

Please forgive anything perceived to be an error.
Where else can this idea be applied?

Evolution of an Idea

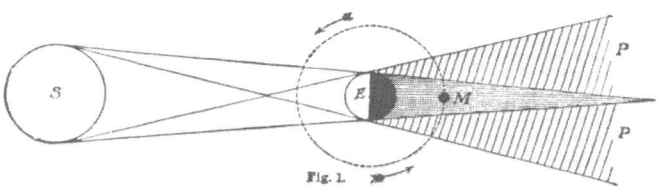

Fig. 1.

This project began as a podcast on January 11, 2017, on the eve of two spectacular celestial events: the Full Wolf Moon and Venus at its greatest Eastern elongation. The project later transformed into **Gratitude & Grace** as you see it now. It was revised in late July 2018, during two other spectacular celestial events: the Blood Moon Lunar Eclipse and Mars at Opposition, in final preparation for publication on November 1, 2018.

To honor my left-handed Grandpop and anyone who is left-hand dominant,
you may wish to reverse the book for a more comfortable journaling experience.

Indigo Sky believes that compassion is our greatest opportunity. But he didn't always feel this way. Years ago, what began as an adventure amongst the stars of Hollywood quickly landed Sky on the streets. Life in Los Angeles felt more like living on a foreign planet. Things were so tough for so long, he wondered if he'd survive. It was then that a new journey began to emerge from the stars above.

A twist of fate and a leap of faith activated another world within. Moments of mindfulness elevated Sky beyond his racing thoughts, giving way for the rise of a fortuitous path with many important lessons. In this place, there was more than just wounds and suffering. There was peace.

Learning mindfulness changed his mind, literally. It allowed Sky to notice two minds; one that secretly seeks to destroy and another where only Love is real. One of the most powerful lessons Sky now knows is that gratitude is the parent of grace and both are to be enjoyed.

This journey inspired a radical metamorphosis, sparking a new odyssey that launched Sky to endeavor to be an explorer of light. He now has the understanding that the path to enlightenment begins with a simple shift in awareness. As he continues his mystical journey, he aspires to be a challenger of his shadows, so he may soften them.

Indigo Skylab presents tools to honor the Divine connection to the heart and soul, to cultivate mindful expression and to assist with setting the tone so life may be enjoyed even more deeply.

Indigo Sky is an empath
who has learned how to be a
diviner of tarot and oracle cards
and his own creation, **ZENpal**™

Certifications thus far include
Reiki, Certified Angel Card Reader™

@IndigoSkylab
IndigoSkylab.com
IndigoSkylab@gmail.com

Give the Gift of Gratitude & Grace

Order anytime at IndigoSkylab.com

Share the book with family and friends or
anyone beginning a new journey who may
enjoy daily reminders for a wonderful day!

Please write a review of *Gratitude & Grace.*

It would be so wonderful to see a fun pic of
you enjoying the book! @IndigoSkylab

Tea and sound bowls while proofing an early draft.
#Gratitude&Grace #Peace #Love #IndigoSkylab

Thank you for your support!
Wishing you Love & Light, today and every day.

References

Abraham-Hicks ℗ by Jerry & Esther Hicks / AbrahamHicks.com / (830) 755-2299
G-SERIES WINTER, 2002 SAVOR THE MOMENT! and 4 CD Album, Boston, MA 9/25/10
Page 14, 24, 38

For more information about Mother Teresa, visit www.MotherTeresa.org
Page 16

For information on The Dalai Lama, Buddhism and their approach to World Peace, visit
www.DalaiLama.com
Page 16, 46, 74

The material in this book is inspired by A Course in Miracles ℗, the Third Edition, 2007. Quotations
are used with permission from the copyright holder and publisher, the Foundation for Inner Peace,
P.O. Box 598, Mill Valley, CA 94942-0598
www.acim.org and info@acim.org.
Page 18, 82, 84

Oprah Winfrey quote used by permission and license. Material Courtesy of Harpo, Inc
Page 48

Special Thanks to Academy Award® Winner Geena Davis for use of quote
Page 48

Special Thanks to Chris Etscheid for being the inspiration behind 'order your day sunny side up'
Page 54

The Holy Bible, English Standard Version® (ESV®)
℗ 2001 by Crossway, a publishing ministry of Good News Publishers.
Page 58

For more information about the origins of the Serenity Prayer, visit the website below.
http://archives.yalealumnimagazine.com/issues/2008_07/serenity.html
Page 86

For more information about Eleanor Roosevelt, visit www.FDRLibrary.org
Page 88

Quote used by permission of Tom Peters. Read more at www.TomPeters.com
Page 98

For more information about Chief Oren J. Lyons and more resources, visit www.worldwisdom.com
Page 102

Quote from Angel Bright used by permission of Jeff Rees Jones, Author & Artist
Page 112

Aloha Font by Rémi Godefroid appears via licensing agreement on front cover and interior

Sprinkles Colors Font by Desiree Gomez appears via licensing agreement on back cover and interior

Graphics and sketches appear via licensing from www.VectorStock.com

नमस्ते
Namaste